WHAT I REMEMBER MOST

BY EILEEN PATRICE
ILLUSTRATED BY TAYLOR GORDON-WOOD

Dedication

For my brother Charlie,
With gratitude to have shared these fond memories with you.

Special thanks to:

Taylor Gordon-Wood for her amazing illustrations and capturing exactly what I requested, Erika Ruggiero for her superb layout work once again, Kathryn Rose for the recommendation to utilize wiseHer consulting services in my writing endeavours, and to my husband Vince and friends Amy, Linda, Tabitha, and Michelle for their honest input and support!

And lastly, to Ali Shelley who graciously made her editing abilities aware to me and offered her services. We make a great team. Here's to more collaborating!

Other books by Eileen Patrice:

Daddy Would Be Proud

*Narrative Non-fiction coming soon

GRANDPARENT VISITS

GRANDPARENT VISITS

What I remember most about visiting my grandmother nearby,
were the chocolate chip cookies fresh out of the oven and piled high.
She lived in the country in Connecticut, with forests as far as you could see.
There was even a circular swing hanging from a big oak tree.
We loved her family picnics, and often played a game of wiffle ball.
Sometimes we played kick the can, and cards inside when the rain would fall.

On Labor Day Weekend, we always attended the big town fair
with lots of animals, fun rides, and a smell of popcorn in the air!
One weekend I slept over and she taught me how to bake.
The bread smelled heavenly in the oven, even better than a cake!

Our other grandparents lived in New York. It was a three hour drive.
They always looked forward to our visits, and couldn't wait for us to arrive!
A little amusement park was near their home, just a stone's throw away.
When Nana told us we could go there, we'd always scream, "Hooray!"
Mom rode the roller coaster with us, on our own we rode the boats.
We never wanted to take breaks, except for root beer floats!

Nana's pot roast dinner had this aroma you couldn't ignore.
Everyone got excited smelling it the second we walked in the door!
With our Grandpa, we played dominoes, and he taught us a card trick or two.
My brother and I learned quite quickly and the time just really flew!

We traveled into the city for the famous Thanksgiving Day parade.
Looked up with awe and wonder, as huge character balloons swayed!
Often Nana saved bread to feed the ducks at the local pond.
Another activity of which my brother and I were quite fond.

Visiting each set of grandparents was always a delight.
On the car rides home we'd fall asleep late into the night.
With full bellies from their yummy food and happiness on our faces,
no wonder we mentioned them when naming some of our favorite places!
It was often hard to leave, and evident we wanted to stay.
In fact, these visits helped make us who we are today.

SANTA WAS HERE!

SANTA WAS HERE!

What I remember most as a kid on Christmas morning,
was my brother running into my room to wake me without warning.
"Santa was here!" he'd shout as he jumped up and down on my bed.
I'd wake with a giggle saying, "Careful, don't land on my head!"

I could smell the coffee brewing as the stereo played a Christmas song.
My brother and I laughed and rolled our eyes as our Dad sang along!
We went to our advent calendar to open Christmas Day,
and smiled when it revealed a picture of Santa in his sleigh!

Downstairs we went to the tree with presents underneath it galore.
"New bikes, how lucky are we? It's just what we asked for!"
With every gift opened and wrapping paper strewn all about,
it was clear our favorite day was this one, there wasn't any doubt.

After Christmas visits we settled in, and Mom began to cook.
Our dog played with her favorite gift, and Dad read his new book.
We sat down for dinner excited, hungry, and ready to eat.
Turkey with gravy, mashed potatoes, and Mom's casserole as a treat!
As stories were told, we often laughed and reminisced,
about Christmases past and the people that we missed.

By night's end we'd sip hot chocolate sitting by the fire,
always feeling this Christmas was better than the ones prior.
We watched our favorite holiday movie, each year our fondness for it grew.
My brother and I took turns quoting all the lines we knew!

As we got older, the love for this holiday never went away.
My brother always acted just like a kid, especially on this day.
He'd jump into my room and tell me Santa finally arrived.
Each and every single time, we laughed until we cried!

BLIZZARD OF 1978

BLIZZARD OF 1978

What I remember most about the Blizzard of 1978
was it made me love snow, it's not even up for debate!
Back in the 1970's - if you didn't already know,
life was very different whenever it would snow.

Early in the morning on any big snow day,
Dad listened to the radio as the school closings would play.
This weather made history - it was that type of storm.
It was way beyond anything considered the norm.

"Stay in bed kids" our Dad explained, "I want you to know,
for quite a while I think you'll play in the snow!"
With school closed for the week, we fell asleep again fast.
What was awaiting us, was going to be a blast!
When we finally awoke our first thought was our sleds.
We whipped off our covers and jumped right out of our beds.

In the kitchen upstairs, we ate our breakfast as quickly as we could.
Ready to go with our coats and boots on, we even pulled up our hoods.
We ran downstairs, opened the door, and in came the cold air.
My brother pushed past me as I laughed saying, "Hey, no fair!"

Big plows came down the street and piled the snow really high.
When we stood on the mounds, we felt we could touch the sky!
We created snow forts and a friendly snowman.
Everyone was outside so we came up with a plan.
Yelling to the neighborhood kids nearby at play,
my brother proclaimed, "Let's have a snowball fight today!"

The next day we went sledding on our neighbor's hill.
We repeatedly raced up and down, oh what a thrill!
After a quick break for lunch of sandwiches and soup,
we hurried back excitedly to rejoin the group.
Even years later whenever big snowstorms would come,
we always wished for them to be just like this one.

OUR TRIP TO THE WEST COAST!

OUR TRIP TO THE WEST COAST!

What I remember most about our first airplane flight,
my brother sat to my left and my mother to my right.
Up into the sky this magnificent DC10 flew.
The pilot greeted my brother, "Hello young man, how are you?"
"Mr. Captain" he said, "may I have your autograph please?"
"Why certainly," replied our pilot with confidence and ease.

We landed in San Francisco excited to be somewhere new,
four cousins we'd never met sat waiting for us too!
An adventure on our Uncle's boat included swimming in a lake.
At one point I screamed, "Was that just a snake?"
"No silly girl" he chuckled, "that's a branch you swam by.
There's no need to make such a big fuss and cry."

Visiting the Redwood Forest was cool, and we also made a fun trip to the zoo.
One day after the movies, I tried an ice cream I could chew.
Bubblegum flavor was an odd and special treat,
after eating it all, my cousin and I blew bubbles in the backseat!
We shopped for souvenirs and rode the famous cable cars,
toured a vineyard and cheese factory, but never saw any movie stars.

Later that night in our cousins' neighborhood, we played hide and seek.
My brother was the winner, but slid and cut his leg - it made me shriek!
A visit to the hospital for stitches quickly put an end to the game.
We still talk of how that slide should be inducted into the Hall of Fame!
My Uncle bought fireworks to celebrate the Fourth of July.
What an absolute blast watching them explode in the night's sky!

Our three-week visit proved more fun than we ever expected.
When it was time to go home, my brother and I sternly objected!
"Can't we please stay a little longer?" Both of us cried.
"Don't worry kids, we'll be back!" Mom said and smiled wide.

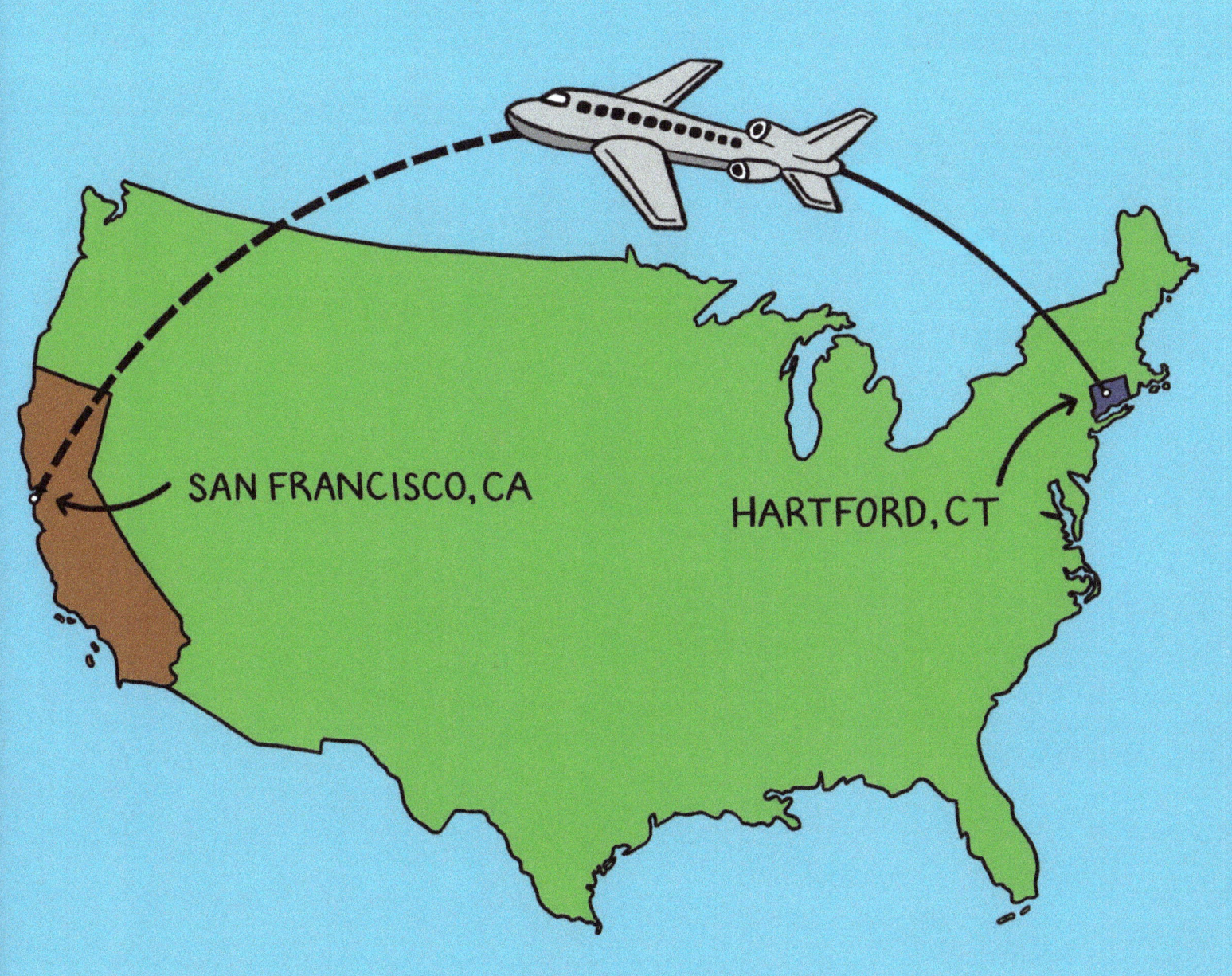

CAPE COD

CAPE COD

What I remember most about our Cape Cod summer vacations:
we'd begin with the lobsters of course, our favorite crustaceans.
We'd feast on them at our rented house, outside on a picnic table.
Seafood was a treat, and always a vacation staple.

Miniature golf was a fun activity and our family had a blast.
My brother putted amazingly, and I loved when I didn't finish last.
There were many beaches to visit and they seemed to go on forever.
Mom packed sandwiches and beach toys - oh, she was so very clever!

We'd take a ride up to Provincetown and pop in and out of each store.
Mom and I loved this part, my Dad and brother thought it was a bore.
One year we went whale watching - way out to sea.
What a great day for viewing them, we counted thirty-three!

An outing in downtown Chatham was best on Friday nights.
That's when everyone would gather for a band concert under the lights.
Other evenings we'd stroll down Main Street, it was calm and serene.
The night would always end with us devouring our favorite ice cream.

Our cousins stayed in a town nearby. We'd visit them and play.
Swimming, bike rides, and go carts – always a fun filled day!
In the evenings, our creativity came alive while producing a little show.
One of us would sing lead, and the DJ was my bro.
Another favorite place to visit was the National Seashore.
The waves grew bigger there than we'd ever seen before!

At the end of each two-week vacation we took one last ride.
Parked at the lighthouse, and we gazed at the ocean's hypnotic tide.
We always knew we'd come back, it's a special kind of place.
Vacations here are impossible without a smile upon your face!

www.ingramcontent.com/pod-product-compliance
Lightning Source LLC
Chambersburg PA
CBHW061751290426
44108CB00028B/2962